e 9 — Words with 'ough' in

'ow'	'uff'	'or'
bough	tough	brought
plough	enough	fought

Any sentence where the word is used correctly.
E.g. When I was ill, I had a nasty **cough**.
    I like to walk my dog **through** the park.
    I like fried eggs, **although** boiled eggs are nice too.
    To make bread, you start by making **dough**.
    You have to be **thorough** when checking for mistakes.

bought, drought, rough

e 10 — The 'f' sound

grap**h**ics, **ph**ase, artificial, so**ph**isticated

frase (phrase), atmosfere (atmosphere), alfabet (alphabet), dolfin (dolphin), fantom (phantom)

elephant, photograph (or photo), telephone (or phone), biography

ction 2 — Word Beginnings

e 11 — Prefixes — un and de

unload, **de**brief, **de**code, **un**safe, **de**hydrate,
unacceptable, **un**mask, **de**construct, **un**do, **un**even,
devalue, **un**appealing

unfair, **un**necessary, **un**kind
Any sentence where the words are used correctly.
E.g. It was **unfair**, **unnecessary** and **unkind** of him to
    do that.

Any sentence where the word is used correctly.
E.g. I need to **defrost** the pizza first.
    Unplug the TV so I can move it.
    You'll need to **deactivate** the alarm.

ge 12 — Prefixes — im, in, il and ir

illegal, **im**prison, **ir**rational

immobile, **il**literate, **in**consistent, **ir**relevant, **im**personal,
impolite, **il**logical, **im**patient, **im**mortal, **in**appropriate

irresistible (irresistible), imconvenient (inconvenient),
imcapable (incapable), inpossible (impossible),
inlegible (illegible)

ge 13 — Prefixes — auto, trans, bi, tri and semi

transport, **bi**plane / **tri**plane, **semi**circular, **auto**pilot,
tripod, **semi**conscious

transform, **semi**colons, **auto**biography, **bi**lingual,
semiprofessional

3. Any sentence where the word is used correctly.
    E.g. The netball team had finally reached the **semifinals**.
        The fans queued to get David Beckham's **autograph**.
        Harry pedalled his **tricycle** round the garden.

Page 14 — Prefixes — aero, micro, super, sub, inter

1. microphone, submarines, microwave, interlocking,
   supernatural

2. submerge, international, microscope, aeroplane

3. Any sentence where the word is used correctly.
   E.g. The teacher turned on the **interactive** whiteboard.
       When I grow up, I want to be a **superhero**.
       The cashier added up the **subtotal** on the till.

Page 15 — Prefixes — tele, mis, anti, photo, circum

1. television, antisocial, misplaced, circumstance

2. **anti**biotics, **circum**navigate, **tele**port, **mis**spelt, **anti**freeze

3. **photo** — e.g. photograph, photographer, photocopied,
   photosynthesis, photogenic, photosensitive.
   mis — e.g. misinterpret, mistrust, mistake,
   misunderstood, mischief, misconduct.
   tele — e.g. telescope, telephoto, televise, telegraph,
   telepathic, telegram.
   anti — e.g. antivirus, anticlimax, anticlockwise,
   antiseptic.
   circum — e.g. circumspect, circumvent, circumference,
   circumstantial.

Page 16 — Hyphenating prefixes

1. E.g.
   co-ordinate — to make things work well together.
   re-evaluate — to assess the worth of something again.
   post-war — after a war.
   co-operate — to work together.
   pre-election — before an election.

2. re-covered, recovered, resent, re-sent

3. ex-champion, co-own, re-establish, pre-eminent,
   semi-detached, pre-school, re-emerge, non-combat,
   anti-aircraft, non-existent

Section 3 — Word Endings

Page 17 — Words ending in 'cial' and 'tial'

1. substantial, artificial, initial, commercial, essential

2. par**tial**, ra**cial**, benefi**cial**, cru**cial**, so**cial**, finan**cial**,
   poten**tial**, confiden**tial**

3. spetial (special), torrencial (torrential), fatial (facial)
   Any paragraph where the words are used correctly.
   E.g. Donna could see from Sophie's **facial** expression
       that she didn't want to go outside in the **torrential**
       rain. It was a shame because Donna had planned
       a **special** day out.

Spelling

Page 18 — Words ending in 'ent' and 'ant'

1. comm**ent**, anci**ent**, extravag**ant**, gi**ant**, inhabit**ant**, appar**ent**, argum**ent**, arrog**ant**, accid**ent**

2. relevent (relevant), differant (different), elegent (elegant)

3. pres**ent**, apartm**ent**, rod**ent**
   Any sentence where the words are used correctly.
   E.g. Finding a **rodent** in the new **apartment** wasn't an ideal house-warming **present**.

4. brilli**ant**, obedi**ent**
   instrum**ent**, tal**ent**
   sil**ent**, eleph**ant**

Page 19 — Words ending in 'ance', 'ancy', 'ence' and 'ency'

1. resistence (resistance), tendancy (tendency), differance (difference), confidance (confidence), efficiancy (efficiency)

2. Any sentence where the word is used correctly.
   E.g. There was a job **vacancy** at the local shop.
   In France, they use a different **currency**.
   He didn't even have the **decency** to call.

3. refer**ence**, hindr**ance**, perform**ance**, intellig**ence**

Page 20 — Words ending in 'ous'

1. fureous (furious), mischiefous (mischievous), couragous (courageous), marvelous (marvellous)

2. serious, hideous, curious, obvious

3. Any sentence where the word is used correctly.
   E.g. He is an **adventurous** boy.
   I want to be **famous**.
   The film was very **humorous**.
   It was a **disastrous** trip.

Page 21 — Words ending in 'cious' and 'tious'

1. fero**cious**, nutri**tious**, cau**tious**, pre**cious**, lus**cious**, cons**cious**, atro**cious**, supersti**tious**, scrump**tious**

2. Any sentence where the word is used correctly.
   E.g. The doctor was worried that the disease was **infectious**.
   I was **unconscious** for two minutes when I banged my head on the cupboard door.
   The cake that Rita made for my birthday was **delicious**.
   The characters in the book were entirely **fictitious**.
   Kylie had a **malicious** look in her eyes as she threw the ball at her sister.

3. gra**cious**, ambi**tious**, vi**cious**, suspi**cious**, spa**cious**

Page 22 — Words ending in 'able' and 'ible'

1.

Ends in able	Ends in ible
enviable	credible
probable	sensible
identifiable	reversible
reliable	terrible

2. vegetable, edible, adorable

3. uncomfortible (uncomfortable), possable (possible), visable (visible), unacceptible (unacceptable)

Page 23 — Words ending in 'ably' and 'ibly'

1. impossably (impossibly), suitibly (suitably), respons (responsibly), incredably (incredibly)

2. miser**ably**, consider**ably**, horr**ibly**, unbeliev**ably**, understand**ably**.

3. arguibly (arguably), noticeibly (noticeably)
   Any paragraph where the words are used correctly.
   E.g. It was **arguably** the best match they'd ever seer team had **noticeably** improved their tactics.

Page 24 — Words ending in 'al', 'el' and 'le'

1. parall**el**, gradu**al**, leg**al**, approv**al**, ais**le**

2. magicel (magical), parcle (parcel), channal (channe medicle (medical)

3. bicycle, capital, kettle, uncle, tunnel

Page 25 — Words ending in 'sure' and 'ture'

1. plea**sure**, lec**ture**
   adven**ture**, punc**ture**
   un**sure**, frac**ture**
   tempera**ture**, moi**sure**
   recap**ture**, enclo**sure**

2. mea**sure**, cul**ture**, lei**sure**, na**ture**, ges**ture**, mix**ture**, expo**sure**, trea**sure**, furni**ture**, as**sure**, architec**ture**, i

3. Any sentence where the word is used correctly.
   E.g. The manager lost his **composure** when his team lost 13-0.
   A famous artist had made a **sculpture** for the pa
   Your blood **pressure** increases during exercise.

Pages 26 and 27 — Words ending with a 'shun' sou

1. physi**cian**, politi**cian**, atten**tion**, affec**tion**, revolutio education, electri**cian**, construc**tion**, magi**cian**

2. pasion (passion), admision (admission), conclusion (conclusion), percusion (percussion)

3. admir**ation**, expect**ation**, prepar**ation**, observ**ation**, inform**ation**

Spelling

posi**tion**, exten**sion**, beauti**cian**, propor**tion**, persua**sion**, techni**cian**, colli**sion**

explo**sion**, confu**sion**
fic**tion**, ac**tion**
permis**sion**, televi**sion**
politi**cian**, magi**cian**

subtraction, musician, collection, confession, punctuation, optician

Any sentence where the word is used correctly
E.g. My grandfather collected his **pension** yesterday.
The world's **population** is increasing.
There was a lot of **tension** before the performance.

ge 28 — *Words ending in 'en' and 'on'*

accordi**on**, gard**en**
skelet**on**, childr**en**
wooll**en**, butt**on**
opini**on**, bat**on**
molt**en**, gold**en**

stalli**on**, cany**on**, citiz**en**, horiz**on**, soft**en**

Any sentence where the word is used correctly.
E.g. They had built a new **prison** just outside of the town.
Sarah had **spoken** to a lot of new people at the party.
The soldier had his **weapon** out in case of attack.
The wooden floorboards went **rotten** after the flood.

ge 29 — *Words ending in 'er', 'ar' and 'or'*

similer (similar), mirrer (mirror), peculior (peculiar), whethar (whether)

calculator, weather, anchor, popular

engineor (engineer), inventer (inventor), collectar (collector), circulor (circular)

ge 30 — *Words ending in 'ery', 'ary' and 'ory'*

surg**ery**, lott**ery**, libr**ary**, dormit**ory**, sal**ary**, hist**ory**, bound**ary**, crock**ery**, batt**ery**, vocabul**ary**, categ**ory**, brav**ery**

grocary (grocery), necessery (necessary), factery (factory), military (military)

arch**ery**, extraordin**ary**
imagin**ary**, di**ary**
discov**ery**, observat**ory**
celebrat**ory**, vict**ory**
myst**ery**, robb**ery**

ge 31 — *Suffixes — 'ly', 'ful' and 'ness'*

dirtiness, painful, hopeful, gently, emptiness, finally

actually, heavily, skilful

happiness, plentiful, wilful, wholly, friendliness, partially, tiredness, coolly

Pages 32 and 33 — *Suffixes — 'ing' and 'ed'*

1. shuting (shutting), amazeing (amazing), shoping (shopping), chating (chatting)
2.

Word	Clue
beginning	The start of a story.
living	Not dead.
winning	Coming first in a race.
timing	Measuring how long something takes.
jogging	Slower than running, but faster than walking.

3. grabed (grabbed), climbbed (climbed), replyed (replied)
4. selling, begging, training, deciding, filming, staring, jumping
5. identified, facing, dragging, steadied
6. marryed (married), cryed (cried), moping (mopping), useing (using), startted (started), smileing (smiling)

Page 34 — *Suffixes — 'ment', 'ship' and 'hood'*

1. sportsman**ship**, state**ment**, neighbour**hood**, space**ship**
2. knight + hood = knighthood
champion + ship = championship
argue + ment = argument
encourage + ment = encouragement
accompany + ment = accompaniment
3. achievement, livelihood, scholarship, dealership

Page 35 — *Adding suffixes to words ending in 'fer'*

1. suffer — e.g. suffe**ring**, suffe**red**, suffer**ance**, suffer**able**
transfer — e.g. transfer**ring**, transfer**able**, transfer**red**, transfer**ence**
refer — e.g. refer**ring**, refer**ee**, refer**endum**, refer**red**, refer**ence**
2. differred (differed), preferrence (preference), offering (offering), referree (referee), differring (differing)
3. deference, inferred, preferable, inferring, deferred, inference, deferral, deferring, different, preferring

Section 4 — Confusing Words

Page 36 — *The 'soft c' sound*

1. convin**c**e, con**c**eal, con**c**ept, **c**ycle, i**c**icle, **c**ircus, suc**c**eed
2. celebrate, princess, immense, evidence, saucepan, consent
3. introduce, juice, influence, recently, exercise

Spelling

Page 37 — The 'hard c' sound

1. crokodile (crocodile), kracked (cracked), eko (echo), cemistry (chemistry), ankor (anchor)

2. Any sentence where the word is used correctly.
   E.g. He was such a **character**.
   Do you play the **keyboard**?
   My legs **ache**.
   Listen to **track** two — it's my favourite.
   There was **chaos** at the supermarket.

3. kitten, mechanic, kitchen, school, clock

Page 38 — Words with 'que' and 'gue' in

1. queue, question, unique

2. Any sentence where the word is used correctly.
   E.g. Kate had to write a **cheque** to pay her landlord.
   Daniel thought the explanation was too **vague**.
   Mary bought an **antique** clock.
   Geoff is a **frequent** visitor here.
   My football team is top of the **league**.

3. guess, guest, tongue, dialogue, catalogue

Page 39 — Noun -ce / Verb -se

1. practice, advice, practise, advise

2.

Noun	Verb
advice	advise
practice	practise
device	devise
licence	license

3. devi**ce**, practi**se**, licen**ce**

Page 40 — The 'sh' sound

1. **sh**ining, para**ch**utes, **s**ugar, bro**ch**ures

2. chef, ensure, issue, session, moustache

3. mashine (machine), preshure (pressure), crached (crashed)
   Any paragraph where the words are used correctly.
   E.g. The **pressure** inside the **machine** dropped, and before we knew it, it had **crashed**.

Page 41 — The 'i' sound

1. tipical (typical), slyther (slither), tryp (trip), oxigen (oxygen), mistical (mystical)

2. Any sentence where the word is used correctly.
   E.g. The psychic looked into her **crystal** ball.
   I love **syrup** on my pancakes.
   They heard a **whisper** from the darkness.
   There was a problem with the **system**.

3. gym, insects, bricks, hymn, lyrics

Page 42 — Words with 'u' and 'ou' in

1. young (or youthful), pumpkins, jungle, double, cou

2. nourished, bubbles, puddles, couple

3. cousins, touch, trouble, southern, country

Page 43 — 'ei' and 'ie' words

1. f**ie**ld, c**ei**ling, rec**ei**ve, ach**ie**vement, fr**ie**nds

2. Any sentence where the word is used correctly.
   E.g. The opposition were hoping to **seize** power in the next election.
   When she was pregnant, Rachel put on a lot of **weight**.
   Thousands of penguins live on the **glacier**.
   Lizzie thought her grandma was really **ancient**.

3. percieve (perceive), reciept (receipt), soceity (societ nieghbour (neighbour), decieve (deceive)

Page 44 — Comparatives and superlatives

1. tall**er**, short**est**
   slow**est**, fast**er**
   old**er**, young**est**

2.

Adjective	Comparative	Superlative
old	older	oldest
big	bigger	biggest
large	larger	largest
angry	angrier	angriest
thin	thinner	thinnest

3. a. Any sentence where the word is used correctly.
   E.g. The maths test was **simpler** than Julia expected.
   I always seemed to be **busier** than my friends.

   b. Any sentence where the word is used correctly.
   E.g. The **hottest** I've ever been was on holiday in Te:
   Dominic was the **silliest** boy in the class.

Page 45 — Unstressed letters

1. diff**er**ent, busi**n**ess, memor**a**ble, bound**a**ry, secretar**y** cal**e**ndar, parl**ia**ment, wid**e**ning

2. volunt**a**ry, int**e**resting, diction**a**ry, fam**i**ly, deaf**e**ning, freed**o**m, fright**e**ning

3. jewell**e**ry, cu**p**board, ras**p**berry, pois**o**nous, lib**r**ary

4. Any sentence where the word is used correctly.
   E.g. The brothers were in **separate** classes at school.
   Basma didn't have a **definite** date in mind.

Spelling

...es 46 and 47 — Silent letters

island, **k**not, **w**rench, s**c**ience, dou**b**t, **g**naw, hand**s**ome

Any sentence where the word is used correctly.

E.g. He created a **scene**.
> Hugh hurt his **knuckle** in the boxing tournament.
> I didn't know the **answer** to the question.
> I stood on a **thistle** as I walked down to the stream.
> I thought of a **rhyme** to help me remember its spelling.

cres**c**ent, solem**n**, s**c**issors, **k**nead

salmon, r**h**inoceros, **k**night, **w**hale

gnomes, crum**b**s, r**h**ubarb, fas**c**inating

silent g	silent b	silent h	silent w
gnarled	subtle	where	sword
gnashed	limb	chemist	wrong
campaign	tomb	exhaust	wrestle

knife, deb**t**, **w**rinkles

...es 48 and 49 — Homophones

too, ewe, cereal, rains, which

there, their, they're

night, whole, scent, sent, knight

Any sentence where the words are used correctly.

E.g. If I **bury** a **berry**, will it grow into a bush?
> My **son** loves playing golf in the **sun**.
> The **tale** was about a mouse that had lost its **tail**.

disgust (discussed), where (wear), sea (see), whether (weather)

warn, heard, sight (or cite), allowed, stair, loan, sale, right (or rite), leak, tide

...es 50 and 51 — Tricky words

Any sentence where the word is used correctly.

E.g. Car exhaust fumes damage the **environment**.
> My dad has two sons, but I am his only **daughter**.
> The charity music concert was a **tremendous** success.
> I need a **mechanic** to fix my broken steering wheel.
> We had the radiators on **throughout** the cold winter.

ridiculus (ridiculous), beutiful (beautiful), priviledge (privilege), nauty (naughty), stomack (stomach)

3. adhesive, psychic, awkward, effects, affect

4. a. interference
   b. preparation
   c. probably

5.

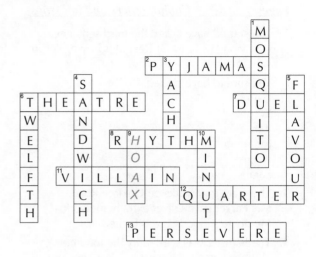

Punctuation

Punctuation

Section 1 — Basic Punctuation

Pages 2 and 3 — Capital letters and full stops

1. You should have ticked the third sentence:
   Last Monday, I saw Dr Reynolds buying sprouts at the supermarket.

2. You should have circled:
   Cairo
   Wednesday
   Italy
   Mr Jacob
   August
   Sarah

3. **T**here are roadworks on **O**aktree **R**oad.
   Mrs **P**arker gave **O**liver extra homework.
   My uncle supports **L**eeds **U**nited.

4. **T**he hamster was startled by the loud noise**.**
   Nobody expected the cake to taste of cabbage**.**

5. **I** am going to **G**reece on **T**hursday**.**
   Or — **O**n Thursday, **I** am going to **G**reece**.**

6. **P**enguins are a type of bird that cannot fly**.** Most penguins spend half their time hunting for food in the water**.** **P**enguins are well adapted to life in the ocean**.** **T**hey can move and see better underwater than on land**.**

Pages 4 and 5 — Exclamation marks and question marks

1. You should have joined up:
   Where is the time machine**?**
   Get out of my room**!**
   The day was warm and sunny**.**

2. The question mark should be joined up to:
   What time is it**?**
   Should we leave**?**
   Who did this**?**
   The exclamation mark should be joined up to:
   Look out**!**
   How amazing that was**!**
   How kind they are**!**
   I'm asking you to sit down**!**
   What a nice shirt that is**!**

3. **W**hy are you hiding behind the door**?**
   Two dinosaurs appeared in my cupboard**!**
   Can you help me carry this piano**?**
   Or — **Y**ou can help me carry this piano**.**

4. I'm so pleased that you've come**!**
   Watch out for falling rocks**!**
   Don't drop the glass vase**!**
   It was the best day ever**!**

5. a. My pet spider has escaped**!**
   b. I don't want to go**!**
   c. Can you open this**?**
   d. Stop making so much noise**!**
   e. Are you going into space**?**
   f. Have you seen this film before**?**

g. My brother is a monster**!**
h. Do you know William**?**
i. Has anyone found my hat**?**
j. That's disgusting**!**

6. Any question where the words are used correctly a[nd] question mark has been used.
   E.g. How did the **elephant** carry a monkey in his tr[unk]
   What kind of **shoes** could you wear with a **purpl**[e]
   Do you think our **neighbour** is really an **alien?**

Pages 6 to 9 — Sentences

1. Statement — A sentence that gives information.
   Exclamation — A sentence that shows strong emot[ion]
   Command — A sentence that tells somebody to do something.
   Question — A sentence that asks something.

2. question
   statement
   question
   statement
   question

3. You should have ticked:
   b. Shut the window before you leave the house!
   e. Don't start playing tiddlywinks now!
   f. Finish your dinner, including the Brussels sprout[s]

4. There were fish in my bed**!**
   I left the room**.**
   They stopped for a rest**.**
   The aliens have found me**!**
   I turned around**.**

5. What time does the play start**?**
   Should we hide the chocolates in the safe**?**
   Mrs Robinson asked if my homework was complete[d]

6. a. Stay away from me. **C**
   b. I go to school every day. **S**
   c. Keep out of here. **C**
   d. Don't do that again. **C**
   e. I've forgotten my own name. **S**
   f. Don't feed the ducks. **C**
   g. Pigs are my favourite pets. **S**
   h. Walk on the pavement. **C**

7. Bees, ants and wasps are insects. **statement**
   Stop talking and concentrate on the film! **comman**[d]
   My favourite subjects are numeracy and literacy.
   statement
   I didn't expect the parrot to start speaking. **stateme**[nt]
   Did you see the hedgehog before you sat down?
   question
   Did you get a chance to see the snowman before it melted? **question**

8. An exclamation mark has been used because the sentence is an angry command.

9. Any statement, question, exclamation and comman[d] where the punctuation marks are used correctly.
   E.g. The badgers are taking over**.**
   Where are the badgers**?**
   What a vicious badger that is**!**
   Don't forget the badgers**.**

10. Any question that makes sense.

Punctuation

Any question that makes sense.
E.g. What are your hobbies?
   What did you do on your holidays?
   Do you have any brothers or sisters?

Any question that makes sense.
E.g. Did they break the plate?
   Did the cat fall into the river?
   Am I feeling tired?

command
statement
question

es 10 and 11 — Mixed practice

Because it is a proper noun / names of
people always start with a capital letter.

Can you tell me how to break into the bank?
My sister goes to judo on Tuesdays.
Get out of the way!
Daniel has blond hair.
Answer my question!
Why are you wearing that silly hat?

Stop interrupting me when I'm speaking!

Any question where the words are used correctly.
E.g. Does your sister have the memory of a goldfish?

command
question
statement
statement

Stand in a straight line!
Our hamster is called Bill.
When shall we leave?

When you're in Rome, you should visit the Colosseum.
It is a huge structure, and it could hold up to 50 000
people. Can you imagine what it would be like to be a
gladiator in such a spectacular building?

ction 2 — Apostrophes and
verted Commas

ges 12 to 15 — Apostrophes

You should have joined:
they are — they're
should have — should've
it is — it's
would not — wouldn't
we are — we're
is not — isn't

You should have underlined:
could've
hadn't
won't

I'm
You're
Didn't
Can't
Might've
Won't

4. **C** — This is Fred's meteor rock collection.

5. You should have ticked:
   a. My car's engine will not start.
   d. They say he's New York's best detective.
   f. Don't go in there — that's the monster's room.

6. Any sentence that's grammatically correct, uses
   apostrophes and includes the words given:
   E.g. That's the hamster's guitar.
       The dinosaur's sister was very friendly.

7. You should have joined:
   The dress that belongs to the girl — The girl's dress
   The dress that belongs to two girls — The girls' dress
   Two dresses that belong to two girls — The girls' dresses

8. My family's house is haunted by a smelly ghost.
   The children's presentation was very interesting.
   Both of my daughters' husbands are terrible cooks.

9.

Singular	Plural
That's my cousin's magic carpet.	That's my cousins' magic carpet.
The tree's leaves are yellow.	The trees' leaves are yellow.
It's dark in the witch's hut.	It's dark in the witches' hut.
The child's toys were new.	The children's toys were new.

10. I really hope **they're** coming to the party.
    I think it is **your** turn next.
    We're going on holiday next week.

11. I'm so happy that **it's** snowing.
    Did you know that **its** eyes are as big as dinner plates?
    Its home is in the rings around Saturn.
    I think **it's** a shame that you're not going to play rugby.

12. You should have underlined:
    Hey, **they're** cheating!
    We're leaving before the yak gets back.
    Your dinner is getting cold.
    What **were** you thinking?
    This is **their** new pet elephant.
    I don't think **you're** helping.

Pages 16 to 19 — Inverted commas

1. You should have ticked the first sentence:
   "Step away from the cabbage!" he shouted.

2. You should have ticked:
   a. "Look out!" she shouted, "There's a giant mole!"
   d. Sally grumbled, "I'll take Scamp for a walk later."
   You should have corrected:
   b. "You'll call me?" Mum asked, "After five o'clock?"
   c. "I hope that goblin knows the way," she sighed.

3. Jeanne was disappointed with her performance today.
   She explained, "I just don't think I was able to shoot as
   well as I expected," before adding, "I'll have to try harder
   next time."

4.

"Don't leave me at home!"	I told her not to leave me at home.
"I won't sulk," she grumbled.	She grumbled that she wouldn't sulk.
She said the troll was not invited.	"The troll is not invited." she said.

Punctuation

5. Any sentence that is similar to these, grammatically correct and contains direct speech:
"The house was painted tartan," I said.
"Can you wait for me in the car park, Raj?" I asked.
"I want to be an astronaut," he said.

6. Any sentence that's grammatically correct, uses direct speech and includes the words given:
E.g. "Your spell is made from snails!" roared the wizard.

7. Any set of sentences that is similar to these:
"That's the biggest fire that I have ever had to deal with," said the fireman. "I've been fighting fires for 15 years, but I can't remember one that was so fierce."

8. You should have joined:
"I've got maths on Monday morning." — direct speech
He told me that he really likes snail soup. — reported speech
She said she was going to Paris in March. — reported speech
"I want to ride on the steam engine!" — direct speech

9. Any sentence that is similar to this:
Nico shouted that a monkey had stolen his glasses.

10. Any sentence that's grammatically correct, uses reported speech and includes the words given:
E.g. The kangaroo asked Sunil if he had seen her friend.

11. Anything similar to this:
You can tell that this sentence is reported speech because it doesn't have any inverted commas.

12. Any sentences similar to these:
Karim complained that he had never been to ancient Egypt and he asked his mother if she could take him.
Karim promised that he would behave, reminding his mother that he was good with the dinosaurs.

13. Any sentences similar to these:
Claire asked Sachin if he enjoyed his holiday in Africa.
Sachin replied that he did and that he saw a lion.
Claire asked Sachin if he was scared.
Sachin replied that he wasn't, as the lion was friendly, and he gave it a sandwich.

Pages 20 and 21 — Mixed practice

1. "Great! It's beans and jelly for dinner tonight," Wayne thought, "and that's my favourite meal!"

2. Any sentence that's grammatically correct, uses direct speech and includes the words given:
E.g. "You're going to ride on your bike," he said.

3. You should have joined:
I — 'm
could — n't
won — 't

4. could've — could have
didn't — did not
I'll — I will
won't — will not

5.

Reported Speech	Direct Speech
He said he was going to the park.	"I'm going to the park," he s
He said he needed time to think.	"I need time to think," he s
I said that I would arrive soon.	"I'll arrive soon," I said.
She told me that she liked geese.	"I like geese," she said.

6. "When are we going to get there?" he asked. "I'm

7. **Hannah's** mum stayed up all night preparing her **daughter's** surprise party. She'd made a beautiful c **its** icing was pink and blue.
"Hannah," she called up the stairs, "could you co the kitchen, please?"

Section 3 — Commas

Pages 22 to 25 — Commas

1. I couldn't find my hat, my gloves or my satchel.
I would like a pen pal from Mexico, Spain or Colo
My sister took me to the ice rink, the cinema and t restaurant.

2. I always carry a pencil, a piece of string, a compas a pound coin in case of emergencies.

3. Sean, Phil, Mike and Paula chased the llamas.
Chips, pizza and spaghetti are my favourite foods.
Andy, Diane and Caroline took their dog for a wal

4. In the countryside, there are lots of animals.
Because of the snow, we can't get to school.

5. After she had left, they went to the shops.

6. You should have ticked the second sentence:
Although they were very hungry, they wouldn't eat sausages.

7. The sentence should read:
Despite trying really hard, she couldn't find my tor who is 84 years old.

8. You should have circled:
Are you going to eat, Rob?

9. In the first sentence, the dogs like eating bark (from and playing, whereas in the second sentence, the d like eating, barking and playing.

10. While Rina drew, her little brother painted.
Ed couldn't swallow, his tonsils hurt and his ears ac

11. Martin's dad, who has always been lucky, won the yesterday.

12. Tracy, **who is my best friend**, told me I should go.
My house, **which has a blue door**, is near the canal

13. My aunt, who is very kind, took me to the cinema.
The book I'm reading, which is about outer space, red cover.
Owen's favourite jumper, which has dinosaurs on it made of wool.

es 26 and 27 — *Mixed practice*

You should have circled:
Commas are used to separate items in a list.
You can use a pair of commas to surround extra information.
Commas can help to avoid ambiguity in a sentence.

These sentences are correct:
I had steak and chips for my dinner.
The town hall's brass bell rings four times every hour.
These sentences need commas:
After snooker, pool is my favourite game.
Carmen plays the banjo, the piano and the guitar.
I locked my bicycle, which is blue and green, by the factory.
Sir, Zoe, the girl with black hair, won't stop singing.

Any sentence that's grammatically correct, and fits with the words and the punctuation given:
E.g. This cat, who is called Monty, has ears which are small, black and pointy.

Although I enjoy it, being a farmer isn't easy. You have to be fit, healthy and strong. Even when the weather is bad, the best thing about the job is being outdoors. Every day I look after my sheep, pigs, chickens and geese.

Although it takes a while, you have to learn how the different pieces move. Monsters, trolls and sorcerers can all move right across the board in one go, but the giant can only move one square at a time.

ction 4 — *Brackets, Dashes*
d Hyphens

ges 28 and 29 — *Brackets for extra information*

Mozart **(1756-1791)** is my favourite composer.
My dad's car **(a Morris Minor)** is very noisy.
There's more information about catching vampires later in the book **(see page 21)**.
We cycled through three counties **(Kent, Surrey and Essex)** in three days.

You should have circled:
Brackets always come in pairs.
If you take all of the words in the brackets away, it should still leave a proper sentence.

I always buy a newspaper (The Gazette) and a book of stamps.
The dog (a spaniel) had memorised his speech about biscuits.
"There's a book on climbing (I think it's by Erica Smyth) by the door."
There are thirteen routes (three of them difficult) through the woods.

Mark tells lots of stories (some of them are true!).
My birthday (the 1st June) is always sunny.
The winning ticket (number 452) belonged to an alien.

5. After we left you, the journey took ages (the flight was delayed). Straight after breakfast (cold meat and rolls), we headed down to the beach. After going sunbathing (it was thirty-two degrees!), we found a little coffee shop and had some cake.

6. Any sentences that are grammatically correct, and fit with the words and the punctuation given:
It was in the summer of 1846 (**a wonderful year!**) that I first learnt to talk to the animals.
The last day of term (**21st July**) can't come too soon.
Mrs Mox (**my best friend's mother**) is sleeping in the corner.

Page 30 — *Dashes for extra information*

1. Losing your shoes — even old shoes — is foolish.
Tia — I can't stress this enough — was the real winner.
Those cats — the ones over there — smell of mint.

2. The sentence should read:
Lucky old Jermaine — the Jermaine who works at the chip shop — got to take me to bowling.

3. Any sentence that's grammatically correct, and fits with the words and the punctuation given:
E.g. You can never tell what Henry **— the naughty boy who lives down the road —** will get up to next.

Page 31 — *Single dashes and bullet points*

1. I'm not sure who did it — it was someone in this classroom.
We had done all we could — it was time to go home.
They had disguises — they were dressed up as pirates.

2. The sentence should read:
"I think you should drink milk — I've drunk it all my life."

3. You should have ticked:
They're used at the start of different items in a vertical list, like this one.
They're used to separate points in a long text so it's easier to read.

Pages 32 and 33 — *Hyphens*

1. You should have circled:
a man-eating tiger

2. You should have underlined:
return
refuse
re-cover
recall

3. I made a last-minute dash.
Auntie Michelle has a cream-coloured coat.
Charlie's a mouse-catching cat.
Twenty-four people can fit into each little boat.

4. Answers may vary, but they must include the given words:
I bought myself a first-class ticket.
Uri was a middle-aged man.
Shane had a half-eaten apple in his lunch box.
Jemma was wearing her custard-stained trousers.

5. One-way ticket to Preston

6. Twenty-one people helped to fix my great-grandmother's shed. They had a great time doing it. I helped out by re-covering the roof with felt. Afterwards, we all had some old-fashioned lemonade.

Pages 34 and 35 — Mixed practice

1. You should have joined:
   hyphens — - — to join together two-word adjectives where they might be misunderstood
   bullet points — · — to show the start of different items in a vertical list
   dash — — — to connect two sentences about similar things

2. Millie needs:
   - one egg
   - two or three rashers of bacon
   - a frying pan
   - some cooking oil

   Starting all four items with a capital letter is also correct. Adding commas or semicolons at the end of the first three items, with a full stop after the fourth, is also correct.
   Answers where punctuation has been used inconsistently should be marked as incorrect.

3. The missing mark is a **hyphen**:
   "My dad is a well-known violinist."

4. Any sentence that's grammatically correct, and fits with the words and the punctuation given:
   E.g. a. If you look in the cupboard — **the one in the kitchen** — you'll find the paints you need.
   b. Christmas (**25th December**) comes but once a year.
   c. Alan is very tall (**he's six foot**).

5. The *Alpine* (built in 1994) sailed into Plymouth.
   This has been a great success — you will all be awarded a jam sandwich.

6. It was Phyllis who had the most prize-winning chickens. She won first prize for three breeds (Sebright, Sussex and Dorking), and the grand prize. This is her last year competing — she's decided to focus all her attention on her parrots.

Section 5 — Colons and Semi-Colons

Pages 36 and 37 — Colons

1. You should have joined up:
   . — full stop
   ; — semi-colon
   , — comma
   : — colon

2. We can't come to the party: we are going on holid
   We are still hungry: the shop has run out of sandw
   You will need to bring camping stuff: a tent, hiking and a torch.
   He doesn't like camping: he is worried about spide
   To make the mixture, you need three ingredients: e milk and sugar.
   I have lost my shoes: they went missing from my ro

3. The birds are beautiful: their feathers shine.
   Harry had won the prize: a trip to the moon.

4. You should have ticked:
   We found your house easily: your instructions were
   The sink was empty: all the water had drained out.
   School is cancelled: the teachers are on strike.

5. You should have joined:
   The books smelt funny: they had got damp.
   The film was great: it was full of surprises.
   We couldn't get any: they were sold out.

6. You only need to know one thing: **their heads are made of jelly**. (Also accept 'You only need to know thing: **heads are made of their jelly**.')

Pages 38 and 39 — Semi-colons

1. You should have ticked:
   He's coming tonight; you should wear something n
   Jane was excited; she realised she'd won.

2. My best friend likes making cards; I like putting hat horses.
   I disappeared early; I don't think anybody noticed leave.
   The window was smashed open; there was glass everywhere.
   My mum likes to sing in the morning; my dad does like it.
   The fireman went through the wreckage; his partne with him.

3. They're out to get you; they're on their way now.
   It was very successful; everybody really liked it.
   I love cats; my brother likes dogs.
   We put the old, smelly suitcase; the table, which ha cost thousands, if not tens of thousands; and the wo donkey on the bonfire.

4. They saw a juggler, who was their favourite; a clown threw custard pies; and a tiger who jumped through

   You need to bring spare clothes, in case you get we towel, to dry yourself off; and some old trainers.

   She always made sure that she had her pencil; her rubber, because she always changed her mind; her scissors; and her sharpener.

   We wanted to go to the zoo, to see the lions; the museum to look at fossils; and the bowling alley, so couldn't decide.

Punctuation

You should have ticked:
I want to make sure she is okay; I think I still have her mobile number.
They teach you about baking; I've always wanted to learn more about it.

Any sentence that includes the correct phrases, and uses a semi-colon correctly:
E.g. My friend likes baking cakes; I like eating cakes.
My friend likes rock music; I like country music.

res 40 and 41 — Mixed practice

My cousin Ronny bought some raisins; I found a bag of flour.
She made the cake for everyone; she hoped they'd like it.
He liked eating Brussels sprout lasagne, while she liked starfish strudel. ✔
In the fruit bowl there were apples, bananas, grapes and oranges. ✔
The giraffes got angry; the raccoons were frightened.
He runs a shop; she flies an aeroplane.
Britain faces a serious problem: ninja foxes. ✔
We need three things: frogs, worms and gingerbread. ✔
She was smartly dressed; I was wearing my bow tie.

Jerry couldn't believe his eyes: there were hundreds of kittens in waistcoats on the bus with him. There had to be a sensible explanation: either he was dreaming, he was going mad or it was a practical joke.

Just then one of the kittens said, "My one's made of velvet; George's is silk!"

Jerry screamed and suddenly found himself on his sofa. He must've been dreaming; he knew he shouldn't have eaten cheese before bedtime.

ction 6 — Mixed Practice

ges 42 to 44 — Mixed practice

You should have joined:
"Have you seen my dragon anywhere" — ?
This is a high scoring game. — -
Marta, who lives in Dortmund is visiting us. — ,
It's going to be a long day — .
"What is this tarantula doing here? — "

"Alex — whose birthday is today — is throwing a party."
I have a pet pterodactyl; Jesper has a pet griffin.
I ate a good lunch: a banana, two cakes and a flask of grasshopper soup.

Answers may vary. For example:
I'm going to go bowling, **shopping**, **kayaking** and **fishing**; Duncan — **who lives next door** — is going **hang-gliding**.

a. "He's not going to enjoy it — he'll hate it." ✔
b. **i** love aeroplanes: jets, biplanes and gliders.
c. "There's a snake on your head!" ✔
d. **Its** Thursday evening.
e. "I didn't leave the rhino's cage unlocked.**'**
f. **Their's** no way I'm going to Alaska dressed like this.

5. You should have joined:
Ben asked if he could go outside. — reported speech
Why is your dad hiding behind the fence? — question
Get down before you hurt yourself! — command
"Looks like rain on Venus today." — direct speech

6. "I've had enough; I'm going home**.**"
"**D**ivesh bought three things: chips, cheese and gravy**.**"

7. E.g. "I wouldn't like to play the tuba," said Stefan.

8. I work as a sheriff in a small**,** dusty town called Solitude (about 30 miles north of the Mexican border). In my time, I've dealt with some mean rustlers, outlaws and bandits. One day — maybe seven years ago — one tough-looking lawbreaker challenged me to a fight**:** a pillow fight.
(You could also choose to put a dash in the last box.)

9. The funquabs that live on **J**upiter are a curious mixture of lions and chickens. The funquab has two legs**,** two wings, a bushy mane and a tail. **Its** other features are just as interesting: a beak, whiskers and razor-sharp claws.

Pages 45 and 46 — Proofreading

1. "**R**ight, that's it! Everybody out on strike!" shouted Rex the sheep**.**
"This grass is useless, and I want something done about it!" he bleated from the top of a rust-stained wheelbarrow**.**
Rex (his real name was Burt Jenki**ns**) stood proudly in front of the crowd. The other sheep arranged themselves in height order: tallest at the back and shortest at the front. There was a lot of excitement because Rex was an ex-politician.
"I have several complaints about our grass: it's not sweet, long, green or juicy enough. I demand to know why!"

2. Bryony flew down the stairs, almost tripping over Nathan's scooter.
"Why does he always leave that thing there?" screamed Bryony, pouring milk on her toast and putting marmalade in her tea. This was an important day for Bryony: **i**t was the last day of her SATs, and Mrs Whinge had organised a last-minute class party.
"Did you have exams when you were at school, Mum**?**" asked Bryony.
"In my day," replied Mum (who was known for her sarcasm), "it was all catching dinosaurs and painting in caves**.**"
"I think we'd better be going now, don't you, young lady?" Mum wiped the marmalade from her daughter's chin and picked up her car keys. **B**ryony still had marmalade in her hair, but she didn't care because today was the end of her SATs.

Grammar

Grammar

Section 1 — Types of Word

Page 2 — Nouns

1. a. robot
    b. bun
    c. sandwich
    d. balloons
    e. snowman
    f. jelly

2. car, slime, potato, computer, hair, ogre

3. Any sentence where the words are used correctly.
    E.g. a. The teacher spilt coffee all over her desk.
         b. The climber found the cabin halfway up the
            mountain.

4. kangaroo, tent
    Any sentence where the words are used correctly.
    E.g. We sat in our tent and watched the kangaroo.

Page 3 — Singular and plural nouns

1.

Singular	Plural
monkey	monkeys
glass	glasses
dragon	dragons
potato	potatoes

2. tree — S, clouds — P, bells — P, goose — S,
    gentlemen — P

3. mysteries, feet, wolves, children, sheep, holidays

4. a. His **shirt** is dirty, and his **shoes** are full of holes.
    b. The **guests** have arrived, and the **table** is set.
    c. The **walls** are made of gingerbread, and the **roof** is
       made of sugar.
    d. Sam's **socks** are stinky, but his **trainers** smell worse.
    e. My **cousins** travel a lot, but my **sister** prefers to stay
       at home.

Pages 4 and 5 — Types of noun

1. Common Nouns — General words for things, animals
    and people
    Collective Nouns — Words for groups of animals or
    people
    Proper Nouns — Names of particular people, places or
    things

2. It always has a capital letter.

3. pod — dolphins
    swarm — bees
    pride — lions
    flock — sheep

4. a. Elizabeth, Thames
    b. Rufus, Pacific Ocean
    c. France, Sunday
    d. Mr Mason, Tuesday

5. love, happiness, boredom, jealousy, anger

6. Gertrude — proper noun
    Kenya — proper noun
    herd — collective noun
    elephants — common noun
    Max — proper noun
    wolf — common noun
    pack — collective noun
    car — common noun

7. a. Any sentence where the words are used correct▌
    E.g. Herbert took great pride in his sheep.
    b. E.g.

Common	Proper	Abstract
sheep	Herbert	pride

Pages 6 and 7 — Pronouns

1. me, themselves, they, myself, him, ours, you

2. George and **I** had a cheese-rolling competition.
    My uncle took my sister and **me** on a tour of his
    spaghetti factory.
    Freddie and **I** fell out because I pushed **him** in the
    pond.
    They awarded the prize to Ollie and **me**, and both
    were really proud.

3. a. Ben bought wine gums even though <u>he</u> doesn't ▪
       like <u>them</u>.
    b. Jane liked her brothers, but <u>they</u> were often mea▪
       <u>her</u>.

4. Paul's pizza was much tastier than <u>mine</u>.
    I didn't know the ball was <u>his</u>.
    <u>Theirs</u> was much more expensive than <u>ours</u>.

5. It's their cat — it's **theirs**.
    It's her pen — it's **hers**.
    It's his tricycle — it's **his**.
    It's your idea — it's **yours**.
    It's our money — it's **ours**.

6. a. George
    b. Rosie and Danny
    c. snakes

Page 8 — Determiners

1. This is **an** easy page of maths sums.
    My brother wants to be **an** astronaut or **a** pilot.
    Please bring me **a** loaf of bread and **a** knife.
    Miriam had **a** headache after listening to **a** noisy CD▪

2. a. I play football on Saturdays.
    b. Is there much water in the pond?
    c. My sister is afraid of heights.
    d. I have two rabbits.

3. In (remove '**the**') August, I went to **an** acrobatics di▪
    It lasted for **an** hour, but **the** best bit of **the** day was
    (also accept '**a**') magic show that followed **the** disp▪
    After **the** show, I had **a** cupcake at **the** best café on
    main street.

Grammar

~es 9 to 11 — Verbs

swims, write, grinning, has, sang, were, discover

Poor Ikram <u>tripped</u> over the cat and <u>fell</u> flat on her face.
They <u>enjoyed</u> the concert, but it <u>lasted</u> too long.
When Jakub <u>showed</u> me his pet tarantula, I <u>fainted</u>.
Liliana <u>likes</u> gravy on her chips, but I <u>prefer</u> curry sauce.

Matilda **tells** jokes all the time.
Ed and Ali **have** the same birthday.
Lara **saves** her crisp packets.
I never **do** chores at home.
They **share** it with me.
My sister **eats** cold baked beans.

I like to read horror stories even though I am scared of ghosts.

At Yanika's party, Olivia <u>danced</u> the most. — Olivia
Owen <u>threw</u> the boomerang to Rhys. — Owen
Akash <u>changed</u> the light bulb for his granny. — Akash
Petra's dog always <u>licks</u> her face. — Petra's dog

Spencer waved his arms as he crossed the finish line.
Claire and I sold our old stuff so we could raise some money.
Jo and Sam missed their bus, so they had to walk to school.

Any sentence where the words are used correctly.
E.g. Tamara and Chris want to swim across the Channel.
    Priti and I are going to eat at a restaurant tonight.

Anne <u>might</u> not be in school tomorrow because she's feeling ill.
If only he <u>would</u> answer his phone!
We <u>could</u> be there before 8 o'clock if that is convenient.
Peter <u>will</u> know what to do with the two-legged cat.
I <u>shall</u> let you know what we are going to do.

You should have circled:
Giorgio will feed the pigs later.

Anitchka wondered when her lost poodle **would** come home.

a. C
b. P
c. C
d. P

~ges 12 and 13 — Adjectives

new, expensive, wonderful, blue, happy

My nan lovingly makes the most **delicious** cookies. They are always **soft** and **chewy** in the middle and **crumbly** at the edges. I especially love to eat them when they are **hot** from the oven so that the chocolate is still **warm** and **gooey**.

My drawing of a fish is **better** than yours.
The weather on the school trip was the **worst** we've ever had.
I think Tariq has **more** computer games than I do.

4. fluffy — slippers
   stormy — seas
   strict — teacher
   difficult — question
   hot — soup
   rusty — bicycle

5. One day, Peter decided to hide in his **favourite** toy shop before closing time, so he could spend the night there. When the owner left, he was very **excited** that his plan had worked. First he played for hours with the **latest** games consoles. Then he built a **complicated** race course for the remote-control cars. Finally, he raced around on the **fastest** bikes until he was exhausted, and then fell asleep on the **cuddly** toys. The next morning the shop owner was **furious**. Peter had made a **terrible** mess.

6. Any adjectives which are used correctly.
   E.g. It was a **perfect** day, so I thought it would be **great** to go swimming at the **tranquil** lake.
   E.g. The party was **terrible**. The food was **disgusting** and the music was **awful**. I had a **miserable** time.

7. Any sentence where the words are used correctly.
   E.g. The girl was very **careful** as she poured the **hot** soup into the **yellow** bowls.

Pages 14 and 15 — Adverbs

1. a. spookily
   b. expertly
   c. often
   d. fast

2. Any sensible adverb that fits the sentence.
   E.g. The elephants splashed **happily** in the water hole.
   The students ran **excitedly** out of the school gates.
   The crocodile moved **silently** through the river.
   The magician's assistant vanished **mysteriously**.

3. a. brave — **bravely**
      annoying — **annoyingly**
      careful — **carefully**
      brief — **briefly**
      happy — **happily**
   b. She cut the cake **carefully** into quarters, so each slice was equal.
      The bee was buzzing around us **annoyingly** — it was really irritating.

4. **Sometimes**, my friends and I have arguments.
   I **never** forget to feed my pet goldfish.
   I ate my dinner, and **then** I went to bed.
   I hoped that the guests would arrive **soon**.
   Tracy had no idea what would happen **next**.

5. Sit over **there** and be quiet.
   I like this village — I have lived **here** for ten years.
   Danny looked **everywhere** for his school bag, but couldn't find it.

6. You should have circled **therefore**, **perhaps** and **surely**.
   Any paragraph where the adverbs are used correctly.
   E.g. **Perhaps** he's forgotten to meet us. If he was running late, **surely** he would have told us. **Therefore**, I think we should phone him.

Grammar

Pages 16 to 19 — Mixed practice

1. A word that names something or someone. — **Noun**
   A word that describes how an action is done. — **Adverb**
   A word that tells you what someone or something is doing. — **Verb**
   A word that saves you from repeating a noun. — **Pronoun**
   A word that describes a noun. — **Adjective**

2. **Noun**: teapot, gardener, laughter, apple
   Verb: learn, arrived, cried, suggested
   Adverb: grumpily, nervously, briskly
   Adjective: delicate, shiny, nervous, lazy

3. a. **Verb**: ran, **Common noun**: ball, **Adverb**: quickly
   b. **Possessive pronoun**: hers, **Adverb**: nervously,
      Proper noun: Jo, **Plural noun**: children
   c. **Collective noun**: herd, **Modal verb**: could,
      Plural noun: cows, **Determiner**: The
   d. **Abstract noun**: care, **Verb**: crossed,
      Adjective: busy, **Pronoun**: They

4. Valentina keeps **her** money in **the** freezer.
   I waited for **an** hour, but in the end **they** did not arrive.
   Brutus wished that he **had** not **eaten** the entire cake.
   We **took** the new kayak out on the lake as it was **a** nice day.
   Omar and **I** had to run to the shop before **it** closed.
   They gave Lizzie and **me a** pair of socks for us to share.

5. **travelled**: verb, **a**: determiner (also accept 'article'),
   fear: abstract noun
   picnic: common noun, **sudden**: adjective, **gaggle**: collective noun, **charged**: verb
   patiently: adverb, **the**: determiner (also accept 'article'),
   she: pronoun, **clear**: adjective

6. a. Any sentences where the words are used correctly and which include a circled adverb.
      E.g. We heard a strange noise and looked <u>worriedly</u> at each other.
        Miguel liked to sing <u>loudly</u> in the shower.
   b. Any sentences where the words are used correctly and which include a circled adjective.
      E.g. On his way to school Jamie noticed a <u>strange</u> creature on the path.
        My guinea pig, Chester, is always very <u>happy</u>.
   c. Any sentences where the words are used correctly and which include a circled modal verb.
      E.g. When you get back home, you <u>should</u> do the washing-up.
        Tomorrow, I <u>will</u> get up early.

7. Francine's birthday is next week — we **can** send her a present in the post.
   I **might** be going to the shops this afternoon with Jake and Sara.
   Would you **mind** buying something for her? She loves board games.

8. a. Any sentence where 'match' is used correctly as a verb.
      E.g. He wanted his football boots to match his kit.
   b. Any sentence where 'match' is used correctly as a noun.
      E.g. The tennis match starts at five o'clock.

9. My sister and **I** love riding our bikes. We race each other and ride **skilfully**. She has **a** blue bike and I **an** orange one. Mine is much **better** than **hers**, bu **thinks** hers is the best!

Section 2 — Clauses, Phrases and Sentences

Page 20 — Sentences

1. a. ✗
   b. ✓
   c. ✓
   d. ✗

2. a. question
   b. statement
   c. exclamation
   d. command

3. Sift 120 g of plain flour into a <u>bowl</u>. Break 2 eggs the mixture and <u>stir</u> well. Slowly add the milk and on stirring until all the milk is <u>incorporated</u>. Put s butter in a frying pan and heat it until it melts. The pour in the pancake <u>mixture</u> until the bottom of th frying pan is covered. Cook the pancake for abou <u>minutes</u> until it's golden in colour.

Page 21 — Paragraphs

1. You should have ticked:
   When you are talking about a different place
   When a new person speaks
   When you are talking about a different time

2. A paragraph contains sentences that talk about the thing. — **T**
   A new paragraph doesn't start on a new line. — **F**
   Paragraphs are made up of sentences that follow o each other. — **T**
   Paragraphs make a piece of writing easier to read. —

3. There was a loud crash inside the warehouse as the burglars clumsily fell in through the window. // "E quiet!" the larger burglar, Larry, told his companion // "Sorry," replied John, a skinny man, as he duste himself off. // Meanwhile, across the road, little H Spratt woke up in bed, wondering what all the rack was. He peered out of the window and saw the lig of two torches moving inside the warehouse. He wanted to investigate but he knew better than to pu himself in danger. Instead, Harry called the police // Fifteen minutes later, he stood at his front door a watched as the police arrested the two burglars and marched them outside. // "Good work, young ma the police sergeant said, patting him on the head.

Grammar

es 22 and 23 — Phrases

Very slowly — Adverbial phrase
Blue leather shoes — Noun phrase
Under the stairs — Prepositional phrase

Who owns the pink unicycle? — Who owns it?
We don't like horror films. — We don't like them.
That woman over there will help. — She will help.
I have met many famous pop stars. — I have met them.

very bravely
extremely clearly
too loudly
surprisingly well
dangerously fast

Any sentence where the words are used correctly.
E.g. 1) Last week, I went to the park.
     2) Tomorrow morning, I will have egg and toast.

b. along the tightrope
c. next to the rolls
d. towards us
e. before lunch

Three curious and brave children go looking for gold in a cave, but they are captured by an incredibly evil and powerful witch.

ges 24 and 25 — Clauses

	Phrase	Main Clause	Subordinate Clause
he fell over		✓	
out of pocket	✓		
before we went out			✓
Saturdays are the best		✓	
they jumped for joy		✓	
when we saw him			✓

They drank a lot of water after they had played out in the sun.
If I win the mud-throwing tournament, we can have a party.
We left the room before he could start his boring story.
I fed the pig, while Lucy took the chickens for a walk.
We had to leave the zoo because a hippo had escaped.
When summer comes, we can go to the beach every day.
I don't like swimming outdoors unless it's very hot and sunny.

3. We went to the park because I wanted to play football.
They will make a film after the TV series ends.
As long as the weather is nice, we're going to the fair this evening.
You can sing along if you want.
The music ended while they were dancing.
My computer has broken even though it's brand new.
If she does well in school, her parents are going to buy her a bike.

4. Any sentence where a subordinate clause is added and a comma (if necessary) is used correctly.
E.g. They swam in the sea after they had built sandcastles.

5. Any sentence where a main clause is added and a comma (if necessary) is used correctly.
E.g. a. When he got home, **he ate his dinner**.
     b. **We went for a walk** even though it was cold.
     c. Before we could say anything, **the car drove away**.
     d. **James was upset** because he'd lost his coat.
     e. **I made dinner** while she had a shower.

Pages 26 and 27 — Relative clauses

1. The street where I live is in the centre of town.
Could you pick up the box that is over there please?
Do you remember the time when we went to the circus?
His parrot, which has blue and green feathers, wouldn't stop talking!
Yesterday, I met the man who owns the bike shop.

2. My best friend, **who** lives next door to me, is very funny.
That's the boy **whose** house is really big.
My brother was late for tea, **which** surprised me.
The children loved the lessons **that** took place outside.

3. Any sentence where a relative clause is used correctly and commas are added correctly where necessary.
E.g. The dog **that has white fur** is always barking.
My uncle, **who is really tall**, loves rock climbing.
The classroom, **which was near the hall**, was full of children.
The weather was awful, **which ruined our holiday**.

4. You should have ticked:
This book that I'm reading is very long.
The car which he bought is bright red.

5. I thought the food Tom had made was delicious.
Whitney really liked all the people she had met.
The homework Miss Green gave us is due tomorrow.

6. Any sentence which uses a relative clause and a relative pronoun correctly.
E.g. The postman, who is scared of our dog, refused to deliver our post.
I have a mug that can hold a litre of tea.

Grammar

Pages 28 to 31 — Mixed practice

1. a. When the dog barked, everyone looked up. — statement
   He tried to fix it, but it was beyond repair. — statement
   Stop doing cartwheels while I'm speaking! (also accept .) — command
   Why did they spend the morning in the house? — question
   I went to the party even though I didn't want to. — statement

   b.

Phrase	Main Clause	Subordinate Clause
all afternoon	He tried to fix it	When the dog barked
in the house	I went to the party	while I'm speaking

2. Any question which is written correctly.
   E.g. Why are you still talking?
   Is there anybody there?
   Have you seen my jacket?

3. a. Any sentence where the commands are correctly changed into questions.
   E.g. Can you make my dinner?
   Will you go to your room, please?
   Could you bring me the remote?
   b. Any sentence where the statements are correctly changed into questions.
   E.g. Is Alex tired?
   Are they early?
   Are you busy?

4. The angry milkman — Noun phrase
   Over the hill — Prepositional phrase
   Really happily — Adverbial phrase

5. a. Any phrase where two adjectives are used correctly.
   E.g. the old and noisy computer
   a happy, white horse
   b. Any noun phrase that is shorter than the original phrase and conveys the same meaning.
   E.g. a handsome and talented actor
   the tall, rocky mountain

6. a. Any sentence where a prepositional phrase is used correctly.
   E.g. The cat ran under the bed.
   b. Any sentence where an adverbial is used correctly.
   E.g. Before we left, we checked to see if it was raining.

7. a. ✗
   b. ✓
   c. ✓
   d. ✗

8. a. We went to a museum **which** had a dinosaur display.
   (Also accept 'that' as a substitute for 'which'.)
   We met a man **who** knew a lot about dinosaurs.
   (Also accept 'that' as a substitute for 'who'.)
   b. The display they had made was very interesting.
   We drew pictures of the dinosaurs we saw.

9. You should have labelled the sentences like this:
   (SC) (MC)
   If you let me, I will dye your hair blue.
   (MC) (SC)
   They watch rugby every weekend because they love
   (MC) (SC)
   We have to wait until Suri has woken up from her ¦
   (MC) (SC)
   You're not getting a bigger slice because it wouldn't ¦
   (SC) (MC)
   While she was watching TV, I hid the remote in the cupboard.

10. relative pronoun — who
    prepositional phrase — out of the bowl
    main clause — She opened the kitchen door
    subordinate clause — As Kaye poured herself some cereal

Section 3 — Conjunctions and Prepositions

Page 32 — Co-ordinating conjunctions

1. The volcano was spitting ash and oozing lava.
   I hated my new hairstyle, so I shaved it all off.
   I don't like football, but I do like rugby.
   Are you staying in, or are you going out?

2. Jiten played tennis, and he played cricket.
   I am the oldest, so I get to sit in the front.
   He went to buy turnips, but they were sold out.
   We can walk, or we can call a taxi.
   Henry didn't like the pie, so he didn't eat it.

Page 33 — Subordinating conjunctions

1. Sophie's mother didn't think — that — it was warm enough.
   Rupert's team won — because — they had been practising.
   The match might be cancelled — if — it rains tomo¦

2. Let's stop him before his jokes get any worse.
   Unless she gets a pony for her birthday, she will be angry.
   Although I like tomato sauce, I hate tomatoes.
   I'm not talking to you until you've given me back m¦ lizard.
   Since he went into space, he hasn't talked about anything else.

3. Any two sentences which make sense and use the subordinating conjunction 'because' correctly.
   E.g. I don't want to go to school because I'm tired.
   Theo never tidies his room because he's lazy.

Grammar

es 34 and 35 — Prepositions

under, into, on top of, over, after

One of the following options for each sentence:
My cousin is a pilot and travels all **over/around** the world.
The burglar made his escape by jumping **out of/from** the window.
The climber wrapped her scarf **around/over** her head.
The clown stood **under/at/over** the bridge.

b. opposite — place
c. because of — cause
d. throughout — time
e. around — place

We left the mouldy cheese **in** the car. (preposition)
The champion runner finished miles **ahead**. (adverb)
The purple monkey is **next to** the dishwasher. (preposition)
They were really full **after** the buffet. (preposition)
The rain came pouring **down**. (adverb)

Any sensible preposition used.
E.g. To find the ancient treasure, you need to go a hundred miles **into** the desert. Go east **after** the oasis and then travel **over** the sand dunes until you come to a pyramid. **In front of** the pyramid is a statue of a sphinx. The treasure is buried **beneath** it.

Any sentence where the words and a preposition are used correctly.
E.g. I was so shocked I jumped straight <u>out of</u> my chair. She found something disgusting <u>inside</u> the fridge.

es 36 and 37 — Mixed practice

so, even though, because, for, when, unless, and, but

Co-ordinating Conjunction	Subordinating Conjunction	Preposition
so	when	during
and	because	throughout
but	if	over
or	that	under

Any conjunctions that make sense.
E.g. "Have you seen Karen <u>and</u> Rajesh this morning?" Mrs Tomkins asked. "They were supposed to be having a piano lesson, <u>but</u> nobody's seen them." Eventually Mrs Tomkins left the room. <u>As soon as</u> she had gone, Rajesh and Karen came out from under their desks. They didn't want to go to their lesson <u>because</u> they hadn't practised all week.

Any passage where the words are used correctly and the subordinating conjunctions are underlined.
E.g. Jack left the house in a hurry <u>because</u> he was going to the cinema, but he was running late. He had taken a long time to shower and have dinner. <u>Although</u> he was late, his friend was waiting outside <u>when</u> he got to the cinema.

5. Carol decided <u>that</u> she would walk the dog (over) the hill.
Martha had chickenpox, <u>so</u> she hid (under) her duvet.
My <u>brother</u> is usually very loud, <u>but</u> he was silent (throughout) the whole show.
<u>Although</u> chickens usually have feathers, mine has fur (on) her head!

6. Any paragraph which uses two conjunctions and two prepositions correctly.
E.g. I was going to hide (under) the table, <u>but</u> I decided it was a bad idea. <u>Even though</u> I'm not allowed (in) my sister's room, I hid there anyway.

Section 4 — Sentence Structure and Tense

Page 38 — Subject and object

1. (My mother) is mowing <u>the lawn</u>.
   (Jamie) fried <u>an egg</u> this morning.
   (I) really enjoyed <u>the magic show</u>.
   (My brother) smashed <u>a mirror</u>.
   (Sue) will watch <u>television</u> tonight.
   (Angela) was writing <u>a letter</u> earlier.
   (My father) always does <u>the shopping</u>.
   (Noel) is drinking <u>a glass of water</u>.
   (The elephant) stomped <u>its feet</u>.

2. a. Emilie enjoys playing computer games.
      Jo highlighted the <u>sentence</u> in her textbook.
      Georgie put a <u>poster</u> on the wall.
      <u>Josh and Eliot</u> are going to paint the fence.
      Jessica caught the <u>bus</u> into town.
   b. subject, object, object, subject, object

Page 39 — Active and passive voice

1. a. passive
   b. passive
   c. active
   d. active
   e. passive.

2. The water jug was filled by my sister.
   The tiger was released by the zookeeper.

3. The dog bit my brother.
   Peter caught the ball.

Grammar

Pages 40 and 41 — Past, present and future tenses

1. will compete (also accept 'shall compete')
   knows
   sing
   had
   will laugh (also accept 'shall laugh')

2. a. I went to the pool and I swam ten lengths. Then I jumped in from the diving board.
   b. I will go to the pool and I will swim ten lengths. Then I will jump in from the diving board. (Accept 'shall' for 'will'. Also accept 'I'll' for 'I will'.)

3. Fatima and Ayesha often **go** shopping. Last weekend, they **travelled** by train to Birmingham to go to the shopping centre. They **ate** lunch at a coffee shop and **chose** a birthday present for their dad. They **had** a great time and **agreed** that they would definitely go again soon.

4. Our neighbour **sits** in the bath and sings opera every night.
   Mum **bought** ten tins of beans at the supermarket.
   My stepbrother **passed** his driving test last week.
   My little sister always **breaks** her toys when she is cross.
   Tau **did** his homework yesterday so he could relax today.

5. He **will go** to Mexico to buy a polka dot poncho. (Also accept 'shall' for 'will' and 'He'll' for 'He will'.)
   We **looked** after our aunty's pet ostrich.
   I **get** lots of chocolate on my birthday.

6. Any sentence which makes sense and uses the future tense.
   E.g. Next Sunday, I will go to my grandmother's house for lunch.

Page 42 — Past tense with 'have'

1. If it <u>has</u> been raining, you can jump in all the puddles.
   Even though I <u>have</u> fed the cat, he is still hungry.
   Although we <u>have</u> planned ahead, we might still get stuck in traffic.

2. Cerys **has drawn** a picture of a house and a tree.
   My uncle **has driven** a sports car around a race track.

3. My sister and I **have had** a great day — we **have been/ have gone** to the shops. We **have been** out shopping for a long time, but she **has found** a dress for my party. I **have told** her that I like it, but it's horrible. (Also accept contractions 'I've', 'we've' and 'she's'.)

Page 43 — Verbs with '-ing'

1. Dad **is reading** the newspaper.
   The pupils **are watching** a programme about Africa.
   I **am waiting** for the school bus.

2. Jane <u>is stopping</u> the traffic. Jane <u>was stopping</u> the traffic.
   I <u>am visiting</u> my grandparents. I <u>was visiting</u> my grandparents.
   Philip <u>is taking</u> piano lessons. Philip <u>was taking</u> piano lessons.
   It <u>is raining</u> outside. It <u>was raining</u> outside.

3. The athletes <u>were running</u> around the track.
   Cara <u>was baking</u> a cake for her friends.
   I <u>was chatting</u> to my mother about school.
   Dermot <u>was worrying</u> about his car.

Pages 44 and 45 — Mixed practice

1. a. passive, active, active, passive, active
   b. (The city) was saved by superheroes.
      (The students) performed a play.
      (Kribley F.C.) scored a goal.
      (My finger) was bitten by my hamster.
      (George) wrote that book.
   c. A play was performed by the students.
      A goal was scored by Kribley F.C.
      That book was written by George.

2. Today, I **will finish** all of my homework. Then, I **wi** out with my friend. She **will be** home from holiday **will have** lots of funny stories. (Accept 'shall' for 'w Also accept contractions 'I'll' and 'She'll'.)

3. Last Thursday, I **went** to watch a rugby match.
   Elle **is cooking** lots of food for her party.
   So far today, Chris **has answered** six questions.
   They **play** tennis together every Saturday.
   We must stay quiet until the head teacher **has** left.

4. writing, bought, found, screamed, dropped, eat, giv

Section 5 — Writing Style

Pages 46 and 47 — Standard vs. Non-Standard

1. Any sentence written in Standard English which co the same meaning as the original.
   E.g. I didn't do anything.
        You didn't go anywhere.
        There isn't anybody who knows.
        I can't go on any more.
        Peter couldn't find any clues.

2. I love **those** shoes.
   He showed **them** around.
   Did you ask **them** to come?
   Who are **those** people?

3. a. They shouldn't <u>of</u> been here.
      I <u>dunno</u> where he's gone.
      I <u>ain't</u> got time to do that.
      We couldn't <u>of</u> gone anyway.
   b. Any sentence written in Standard English which conveys the same meaning as the original.
      E.g. They shouldn't have been here.
           I don't know where he's gone.
           I haven't got time to do that.
           We couldn't have gone anyway.

Grammar

We are doing a drawing of each other.
They go to the supermarket.
That was really clever of you.
I have been there loads of times before.
I don't know if **they are** going to win the race.
He was here earlier.

He's doing very **well** at school.
I love that song — it is really **good**.
She mashed the potatoes **well**.
It was a **good** performance.
I **have seen** that film already.
We **have been** / **have gone** to the pool.
Liam **drank** a pint of water.
I **have** only just woken up. / I only just **woke** up.
Elsa **thought** about her essay.

e 48 — Formal and informal writing

That's ace! — That is great.
He'll be fuming, won't he? — Do you think he will be angry?
It's very nippy outside! — It is very cold outside.
I'm really chuffed. — I am very happy.

Jamie'll get here, <u>don't you reckon?</u>
He did say he was coming, <u>didn't he?</u>
She'll phone us if he's late, <u>won't she?</u>
It's a horrible day, <u>isn't it?</u>
Any sentence written in formal English which conveys the same meaning as the original.
E.g. Do you think Jamie will get here?
    Did he say he was coming?
    Do you think she will phone us if he is late?
    Is it not a horrible day?

If **I were** you, I would consider feeding the kitten before it gets angry.

ges 49 and 50 — Mixed practice

Standard English	Non-Standard English
It's all mine.	We was well good.
He's the butcher's son.	They has no idea.
This is delicious.	He can run real quick.
Who wants it?	That are funny.
I would like to stay.	I isn't going back.

Any sentence written in formal English which conveys the same meaning as the original.
E.g. Josie did not think the story was very good.
    Do you think we should buy a lot of vegetables?
    We do not have the time to argue about it.

3. I ain't seen nothing. — I haven't seen anything.
We've never gone nowhere. — We've never gone anywhere.
I don't like them cakes. — I don't like those cakes.
Yous has got a lot to learn. — You have got a lot to learn.

4. It is important that he arrive promptly. — formal
It'd be cool if he got there on time. — informal

5. Any sentence written in Standard English which conveys the same meaning as the original.
E.g. We have been very busy.
    How many people are here?
    You run more quickly than me.
    It isn't a joke.
    I slept really well last night.
    We have done loads of stuff. / We did loads of stuff.
    She was taught differently.

Section 6 — Making and Choosing Words

Page 51 — Word families

1.

Noun	Verb	Adjective
weight	to weigh	weighty
friend	to befriend	friendly
correction	to correct	correct

2. *lovely*, loving, unloved, beloved
reverses, reversed, irreversible, reversing
destruct, construct, instruct, instruction

3. b. circle

Pages 52 and 53 — Prefixes

1. <u>pre</u>historic, <u>un</u>real, <u>dis</u>mount, <u>over</u>heat, <u>inter</u>act, <u>mis</u>treat, <u>dis</u>obey

2. Nima knew a lot about **subordinate** clauses.
My brother had an allergic **reaction** to the nuts he was eating.
Fran wanted to call her friend, but she could not find the **telephone**.
Nick's sister was very **antisocial** and stayed in her room all day.
The children don't **misbehave** in class because their teacher is strict.

3. Dan gets very **un**happy when other people **mis**understand him.
It is **in**appropriate to wear your pyjamas in the **super**market.

4. de — crypt (decrypt)
re — arrange (rearrange)
il — legal (illegal)
in — secure (insecure)

5. It is very **un**likely that there will be an alien invasion.
   Your explanation seems **im**probable, but I'll believe you.
   My dog and my cat are **in**compatible — they're always fighting.
   It was **ir**responsible to let us play with the water balloons.
   Being short is a real **dis**advantage in basketball.

6. **im**practical
   unclear
   imperfect
   unimportant
   unacceptable
   dishonest

Pages 54 and 55 — Suffixes

1. music**ian**, play**ful**, close**ness**, prefer**able**, self**less**, employ**ment**, child**hood**

2. Everyone congratulated Hannah on her wonder**ful** performance.
   Be careful what you eat in the jungle — many plants are poison**ous**.
   Unfortunately, a chocolate teapot would be completely use**less**.
   Ele is a self**ish** person because she only ever thinks about herself.

3. He had to author**ise** the payment.
   She tried not to alien**ate** her friends.

4. E.g. painful, painless, comfortable, comfortless, careful, careless, acceptable, acceptance, helpful, helpless, hopeful, hopeless

5. a. That book was very **inspirational**.
   b. How can you **justify** spending that much money on sweets?
   c. I like my **neighbourhood** because everyone is very friendly.

6. Homework isn't **enjoyable**, but it's **foolish** to avoid it.
   A lion's **powerful** jaws can be **dangerous**.

7. Any sentence where the words are used correctly.
   E.g. loneliness: The film was all about **loneliness** and fear.
   amusement: The group watched the clown with **amusement**.
   election: The politician won the **election**.

Pages 56 and 57 — Making verbs

1. Kate is **walking** her ferret.
   Sam **passed** his dad the salt.
   Fatima **played** in her band last night.
   He **says** he has a time machine.
   Ali always **wins** at board games.
   James is **acting** like an idiot.

2. The stars are **shining** very brightly tonight.
   Ben is **planning** to spend all his money on novelty mugs.
   Sasha wastes so much time **deciding** how to do her hair.
   The farmer's cows are **invading** our garden.

3. Any sentence where the words are used correctly.
   E.g. believed: Lucille **believed** she would be famo one day.
   applied: My dad **applied** to join the tennis clu
   tried: The dog **tried** to chase the cat up the tre

4. hurried, dialled, liked, supplied, banged, flapped,

5.

Verb	-ing form	Verb	-ing form
keep	*keeping*	tie	tying
ride	riding	win	winning
buy	buying	fry	frying
dig	digging	die	dying

6. Any sentence where the words are used correctly.
   E.g. I think my older brother **studies** too hard.
   They all **stopped** talking to listen to the teache
   My cat loves **having** her ears scratched.

Page 58 — Synonyms

1. accurate — correct
   insect — bug
   enjoy — relish
   safe — secure

2. You should have circled the words in bold:
   The rich chocolate cake was so **delicious** that Jo sa she'd never had such an **appetising** cake.

3. Any suitable synonym:
   E.g. tired — exhausted
   wet — soaking
   great — excellent
   handy — useful
   silent — quiet
   thankful — grateful

4. Any sentence where a synonym is used correctly.
   E.g. funny: The clown at the party was **hilarious**.
   truthful: The answers she gave were completel **honest**.

Page 59 — Antonyms

1. pull / push
   high / low
   worst / best
   desolate / populated
   misplace / locate

2. Any suitable antonym.
   E.g. clean — dirty
   fast — slow
   tall — short
   tidy — messy
   bright — dull
   spend — save

Any sentence where an antonym is used correctly.
E.g. The test was far too **easy** for most of the pupils.
    The lift was broken — it could only go **down**.

es 60 and 61 — Mixed practice

walk — to walk — walking
sign — resign — signature
competition — compete — competitive

Word	Prefix	Root Word	Suffix
unbreakable	_un_	_break_	_able_
reworking	re	work	ing
disjointed	dis	joint	ed
inconsiderate	in	consider	ate

I'm surprised that the supermarket was <u>shut</u> — it's usually **open**.

Darren was <u>fortunate</u> not to get caught — he counted himself **lucky**.

Zamira thought the film was very <u>dull</u>, but her brother found it **interesting**.

Put the cat <u>outside</u> — he shouldn't be **indoors** anyway!

Vikram was <u>sprinting</u> towards the theatre where he was meeting a friend.

He was late because he'd had a <u>lengthy</u> <u>discussion</u> with the doctor.

The doctor wanted to <u>prescribe</u> him <u>antibiotics</u> for his cough.

Any sentence where the words are used correctly.
E.g. disappearance: The **disappearance** of the crown
    jewels caused a scandal.
    transportation: Trains are a type of **transportation**.
    impolitely: He spoke very **impolitely** to the waiter.

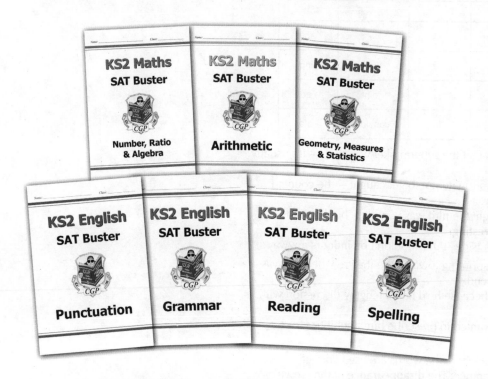